NATIONAL GEOGRAPHIC

T0040060

The Speedy Cheetah

Rachel Elliott

A cheetah is a kind of wild cat.
Cheetahs live in Africa.

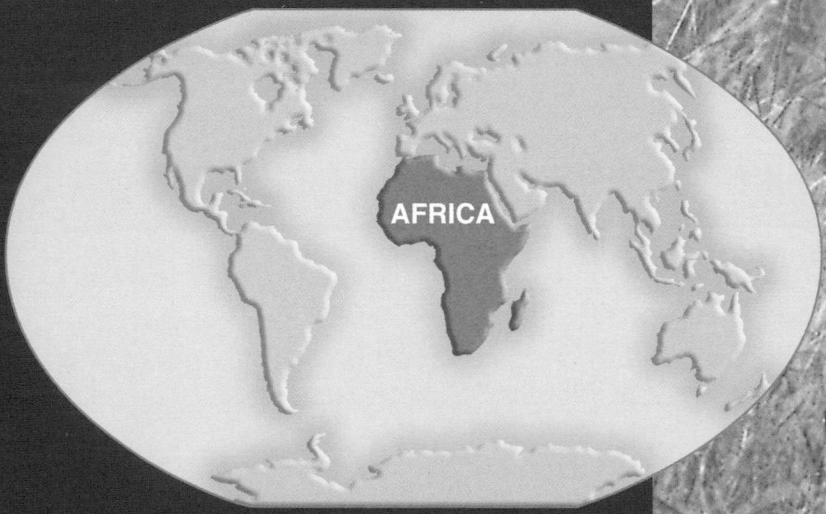

A cheetah looks like a very large cat.
A cheetah weighs about 120 pounds.

A cheetah has a long body.
Its body is about 4 feet long.

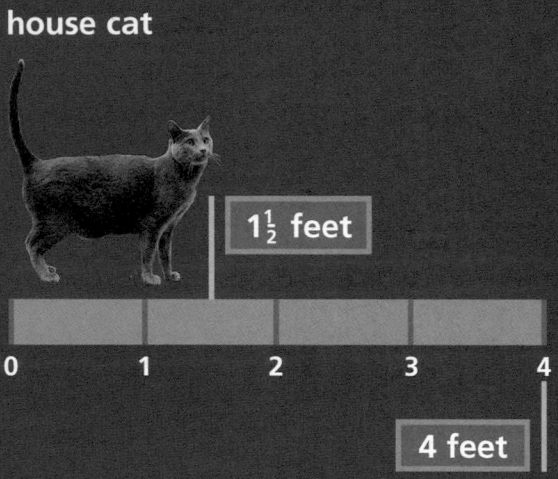

A cheetah stands on 4 legs.
It grows to be about 3 feet tall.

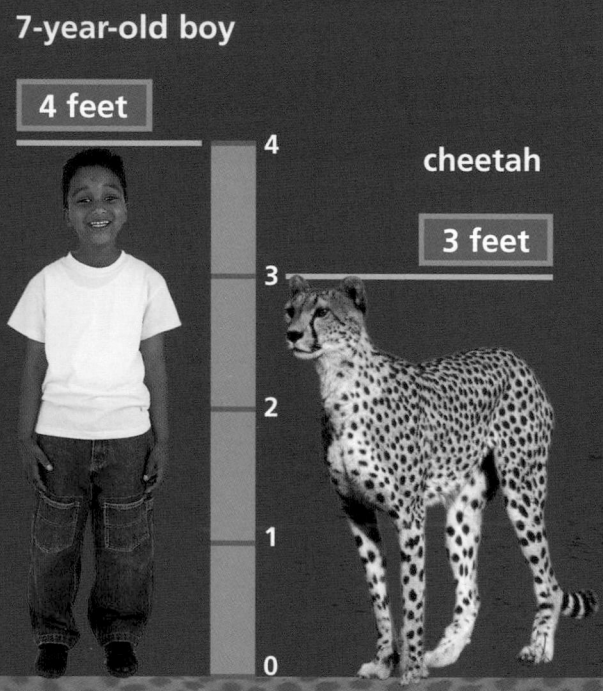

A cheetah has strong legs.
It can run as fast as a car on a highway.

60 miles an hour

Baby cheetahs are called cubs.
The cubs soon grow up.
They become fast and beautiful cheetahs.